In Session with the Jazz Masters

Ella Fitzgerald

FABER *ff* MUSIC

Series Editor: Sadie Cook

Music Editorial & Project Management: Artemis Music Limited
Photos supplied by Redferns Music Picture Library
Design & Production: Space DPS Limited
All songs on this CD are performed by session musicians.
Whilst every effort was made to replicate the style of the original
performances these are not the original recordings.

© International Music Publications Ltd
First published in 2000 by International Music Publications Ltd
International Music Publications Ltd is a Faber Music company
3 Queen Square, London WC1N 3AU
Printed in England by Caligraving Ltd
All rights reserved

ISBN10: 0-571-52832-5
EAN13: 978-0-571-52832-5

To buy Faber Music publications or to find out about the full range of titles available
please contact your local music retailer or Faber Music sales enquiries:
Faber Music Limited, Burnt Mill, Elizabeth Way, Harlow CM20 2HX
Tel: +44 (0)1279 82 89 82   Fax: +44 (0)1279 82 89 83
sales@fabermusic.com   fabermusic.com

In Session with the Jazz Masters

Ella Fitzgerald

In the Book...

On The CD...

Biography

On 2 December 1979, following a reception with America's First Lady, Rosalynn Carter (wife of President Jimmy Carter), the Kennedy Center was the venue for the presentation of five lifetime achievement awards in the performing arts. Along with Aaron Copland, Henry Fonda, Martha Graham and Tennessee Williams, Ella Fitzgerald was bestowed with an award in a ceremony which she described as 'the proudest moment of my life'. Here was deserved recognition for her huge contribution to jazz. It was something that she could never have dreamed about at the start of her career, when chronic shyness worked against her chances of success as a performer.

In 1934 a dare with two friends caused her to enter a talent show, as a dancer, at the Harlem Opera House. This was the venue from which a number of other famous performers got their breaks into the music business, including Sarah Vaughan, James Brown and the Isley Brothers. It was also notorious for its tough audiences, and Ella was understandably nervous as she stepped out on stage. To make matters worse she was following on after another dance act which had just brought the house down. When the music started for her own routine, Ella found she was unable to move, let alone dance. Urged to 'Do something', she responded by beginning to sing *Judy*, a song by Connee Boswell, one of her favourite singers. The band soon joined in and it was a great success with the crowd. Having won over the audience, Ella discovered she had won a $25 prize – 'the hardest money I ever earned', she confessed. It was a real turning point because she now knew that she wanted to be a professional singer. To make this a reality she combined determination and perseverence with the help of two people who really believed in her; Chick Webb and Norman Granz.

Ella Jane Fitzgerald was born in Newport News, Virginia on 25 April 1918, but moved when very young

Photo: Michael Ochs Archives

with her mother, Tempie, to New York State. (Her father had died shortly after the end of World War I.) Ella's first musical influence was her mother singing around the house and playing records. Ella used to earn money by tap dancing in public, and this encouraged her to go for the now infamous audition at the Harlem Opera House.

Shortly after the big break seemed to have arrived – CBS had offered her a recording contract – Ella's mother died, leaving her an orphan. Still entering the amateur night contests at the Opera House, she eventually won a professional contract and appeared with the Tiny Bradshaw Band in 1935 and was spotted by Bardou Ali, the emcee with drummer Chick Webb's orchestra. Webb had to be convinced to take Ella on, but after winning over the Yale audience on the Orchestra's next date she soon became a permanent fixture in the line-up. As she was still an orphan Ella needed legal guardians to start her career officially, so in stepped Chick Webb and his wife to adopt her.

" She had a vocal range so wide you needed an elevator to go from the top to the bottom. "

David Brinkley

The first record which Ella cut with Chick Webb, *Love And Kisses*, was made in June 1935 and within two years she was winning the Down Beat magazine poll as top female vocalist. Then, in 1938, the landmark recording was made of *A-Tisket, A-Tasket*, a song on which Ella collaborated on the lyric. Known as a 'jitterbug spiritual', it immediately became a massive hit and stayed at the top of the charts for an incredible 17 weeks. Undoubtedly due to the presence of Ella, the Chick Webb Orchestra experienced a meteoric rise in popularity, becoming the first black band to play at Park Central Hotel and the Paramount Theater on Broadway.

When, in June 1939, Ella's musical mentor Chick Webb died suddenly, she was cast in the role of bandleader. The Orchestra assumed her name and continued for another two years before a combination of factors lead them to disband. Also about this time the opportunity to be involved in the movies came along and in 1942 Ella appeared in 'Ride 'Em Cowboy', starring Bud Abbott and Lou Costello.

During this period Ella sought to expand her musical horizons and experimented with some different styles. When she came back to jazz, bebop was just emerging as the latest innovation and in 1947 she jumped at the chance to sing with Dizzie Gillespie's band. Adapting to this new style, Ella used her voice as a musical instrument, developing a brand of scat singing that sat perfectly with the improvisations of the players around her, whilst also displaying a versatility which was to become one of her trademarks. Her experience now meant that switching between styles wasn't a problem and she could sing with just about anyone.

The next year saw a chance meeting between Ella and Norman Granz which was to shape her career from there on. Granz asked her to join his Jazz at the Philharmonic tour, which Ella readily agreed to as she was shortly to be married to Ray Brown, the bass player with the group. (Ella had married before, at the age of 23, to dancer Benny Kornegay, but the marriage was annulled within the year.) The tours helped to hone Ella's improvisation skills and in 1954 Granz became Fitzgerald's manager.

Within a year Granz was able to put into operation a plan to broaden yet further Ella's appeal when he succeeded in persuading Decca to release the singer from her recording contract so that she could record on his Verve label. This lead to the milestone SONG BOOK series of albums featuring the songs of Harold Arlen, Irving Berlin (for which she received a Grammy Award in 1958), Duke Ellington, George and Ira Gershwin, Jerome Kern, Johnny Mercer, Cole Porter, and Rodgers and Hart. This series of albums is generally regarded as the definitive version of each composer's material, even prompting Ira Gershwin to comment 'I didn't realise our songs were so good until Ella sang them'.

The advent of rock'n'roll might have lead to Fitzgerald disappearing from the scene, but the passing years only seemed to enhance her

> " The only thing better than singing is more singing. "

Photo: Max Jones Files

ELLAselected discography

Title	Label	Date
Ella And Her Fellas	Hallmark	1938
75th Birthday Celebration	GRP	1938
Ella: The Legendary Decca Recordings (Box)	GRP	1938
Lullabies For Birdland/Sweet And Hot	Decca	1945
First Lady Of Song (Box)	Verve	1949
Billie, Ella, Lena, Sarah	Columbia	1955
The Duke Ellington Song Book (Complete)	Verve	1956
The Rodgers & Hart Song Book	Verve	1956
The Cole Porter Song Book	Verve	1956
The Irving Berlin Song Book	Verve	1956
Ella In Rome: The Birthday Concert (Live)	Verve	1958
The George And Ira Gershwin Song Book	Verve	1959
The Harold Arlen Song Book [Vol 1-2]	Verve	1960
Mack The Knife	Verve	1960
The Intimate Ella	Verve	1960
Ella Returns To Berlin	Verve	1961
Ella & Basie	Verve	1963
The Jerome Kern Song Book	Verve	1963
The Johnny Mercer Song Book	Verve	1963
Ella At The Duke's Place	Verve	1965
Ella & Duke At The Côte D'Azur	Verve	1966
Dream Dancing	Pablo	1972
Newport Jazz Festival: Live At The Carnegie Hall	Columbia	1973
Ella In London	Pablo	1974
The Complete Ella Fitzgerald And Louis Armstrong On Verve (Box)	Verve	1997

reputation as a singer for all generations. Having won more Grammy awards in 1960 and 1962 Ella continued to tour and record, and in the early 1970s was one of the first artists to feature on Granz's newly-established Pablo Records label. The '70s and '80s saw Fitzgerald receiving numerous awards – including Best Female Jazz Singer from Down Beat magazine 18 years in a row – culminating in the presentation of the National Medal of Arts by President Ronald Reagan at the White House in 1987.

Ella's musical delivery and technique have been the subject of numerous studies down the years, but she never received any formal training. Instead she used her God-given talents – perfect pitch, precise intonation, crystal-clear diction and two-and-half octave range – in a way which can only be described as natural. Perhaps what set Ella apart from other singers of the time was her sense of rhythm and the possession of a voice that was unusual in its endurance. Her scat singing, which required a high degree of improvisation, left many jazz instrumentalists in awe of her technique, something remarkable in a person recognised as being one of the shyest in the business, especially when it came to the media.

Despite advancing years there was little discernible ageing of her voice, although Ella's later years were dogged by diabetes, causing her to be virtually housebound. The condition weakened her eyesight and in 1993 further complications meant that she had to have both legs amputated below the knees.

She died at her Beverly Hills home on 15 June 1996 at the age of 78. The following year the Ella Fitzgerald Collection of her entire music library, photographs and videos was donated to the Library of Congress. Amongst the collection's more unusual exhibits is the remains of the glass shattered by Ella's voice in the 'Is it live or is it Memorex?' television advert!

The legacy of Ella's remarkable journey from child poverty to international stardom lives on in numerous landmark recordings. She recorded in excess of 250 albums – probably more than any other artist – and such a legacy dictates that both her contemporaries and subsequent artists cannot fail to have been influenced by her. Would Ella Fitzgerald's name be known to the world if she had auditioned successfully as a dancer? In all probability it wouldn't be, but the dancing career she craved was still evident in her singing because of the natural sense of rhythm and movement which she brought to it. If, along with Elvis, any singer is internationally known by their Christian name alone, Ella is that singer – the First Lady of Song.

BEWITCHED

Words by Lorenz Hart
Music by Richard Rodgers

Bewitched

Bewitched

Vocal Notes

Bewitched

This velvety ballad was originally written by Rodgers and Hart for their show 'Pal Joey' in 1940, and was first performed by Vivienne Segal. In 1957 Columbia Pictures made it into a Hollywood film starring Rita Hayworth and Frank Sinatra.

Oddly the song was initially more successful in France (under the title *Perdu Dans Un Reve Immense D'Amour*) than in its native America. However, the momentum of its European success eventually carried it to recognition in its homeland, prompting a revival of the show from which it came.

Like many show tunes it has become famous as a vehicle for any number of jazz artists, and especially associated with Ella, who delivers a masterclass in subtle delivery, phrasing and timing. Her manipulation of time throughout the song is incredible – she seems to imbue the vocal line with an elasticity that makes it seem almost fluid – as she pours her molten chocolate voice into every nook and cranny of the song.

Here are just a few points to look out for in her performance. First, her intonation. Though Ella does use vocal techniques like scoops, portamento, bends and so on, she never does so to disguise an inability to pitch a difficult interval, as some singers do.

Notice how, in the colla voce intro, her pitching is perfect as she places the notes with the precision of a horn. This certainty of pitch allows her to be much more subtle in her use of decorative techniques, for example in the use of the slightest portamento of the second syllable of 'awake' in bar six.

Ex 1 'like a daisy I'm awake'

Here's another technique that is totally Ella – the vocal shake. This is not unlike the kind of thing a coloratura soprano might do in an operatic aria, but here Ella reduces it to a subtle micro-second of quavering in the voice, though always under perfect control. She displays this brilliantly, and with a mischievous sense of the ironic, in the line 'with no bromo seltzer handy I don't even shake' in bars eight and nine. She puts in two such shakes in the same line.

Ex 2 'with no bromo seltzer handy I don't even shake.'

Now to her manipulation of time. Notice how in the first chorus she plays around with the rhythm of the words 'a simpering, whimpering child again'.

Ex 3 'a simpering, whimpering child again'

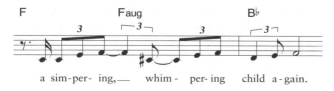

We've notated as much of this back-phrasing as possible without making the music difficult to read, but to understand it fully you just have to listen to it. The subtle delay of a note here, the extension of another across the beat there, and you start to achieve the fluidity of line mentioned earlier. Her control (of both her voice and her musical ideas) allied to an immense, innate musicality allow her to manipulate time in a very creative way.

TECHNIQUEtip

To emulate Ella's shake, try singing one note, followed by its lower neighbour. Do this slowly, with as much control as you can. Make certain you are sure of the pitch of each note. Now introduce a small shake on the front of the second note. When you've got this under control try singing down the lowest five notes of a scale, introducing the shake in different places each time. Then try different scales and different keys.

MY FUNNY VALENTINE

Words by Lorenz Hart
Music by Richard Rodgers

My Funny Valentine

My Funny Valentine

Vocal Notes

My Funny Valentine

This song is an absolute classic that's been covered by many artists in all manner of styles. It was written by Richard Rodgers and Lorenz Hart for the Broadway musical 'Babes In Arms' in 1936, and it's a tune that has stood the test of time. It was re-recorded, for example, by Michelle Pfeiffer for the 1989 Twentieth Century Fox movie 'The Fabulous Baker Boys'.

It is a truly superb lyrical tune that has become a great vehicle for numerous singers and various jazz artists (who can forget Miles Davis' haunting version of the tune?). Here it gives Ella the opportunity to display the rich warmth of her voice, her understanding of a lyric and her beautiful phrasing.

The song falls into two main parts. First there is the colla voce introduction, followed by the main body of the song, and these two elements are treated very differently. In the intro Ella's approach is quite 'throw-away', meaning that her tone and delivery are light, almost casual. She pulls the phrases around, mimicking the rhythms of speech rather than of song, and she lands on the long notes 'par-ade' and 'made' lightly, from above, using a delicate vibrato.

Ex 1 'virtue doth parade'

vir - tue doth pa - rade.——

Ex 2 'picture thou hast made'

pic - ture thou hast   made.

The comic content of the line 'slightly dopey gent' is beautifully played by Ella. She places a deliberate but subtle emphasis on the first syllable of 'dopey', but then eases into an affectionate warm tone on 'gent' before launching into the main body of the song. This is a tricky but rewarding corner in the song, and Ella negotiates it with an assured mastery that sets the standard for this style of singing.

Ex 3 'slightly dopey gent'

Once into the verse she pours on the velvety tone. Her breathing and phrasing are exemplary. Notice how, in bar 23 she alters the tune to make it a descending G minor arpeggio, thus allowing her briefly to get into her middle register on the important words 'sweet comic'. This lightens the tone for this gently mocking lyric – a far better approach than what's written, which is to repeat the tune of the first two bars of the verse.

Ex 4 'sweet comic valentine'

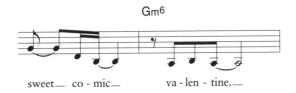

The next phrase (bars 25-28) is a mini-masterclass in ballad singing. The lyric 'you make me smile with my heart' is set beautifully, with the word 'smile' sitting on top of an ascending phrase, and the word 'heart' sitting at the bottom of a gently descending phrase. Each is emphasised by a long note and its relative positioning at the strongest part of the bar (the first beat). Ella takes all these good compositional ingredients and adds a little spice of her own. Listen carefully to the phrase, and notice how she emphasises the word 'smile' with a subtle scoop and a gentle warming of the tone. Now look at the end of the phrase and see how she decorates the last word with a little neighbour-note figure and a lessening of the tone, almost shyly delivering the lyric. It's this combination of vocal talent and ability to deliver a song from the heart that sets Ella apart as one of the greatest ballad singers of all time.

Ex 5 'you make me smile with my heart'

Ev'ry Time We Say Goodbye

Words and Music by Cole Porter

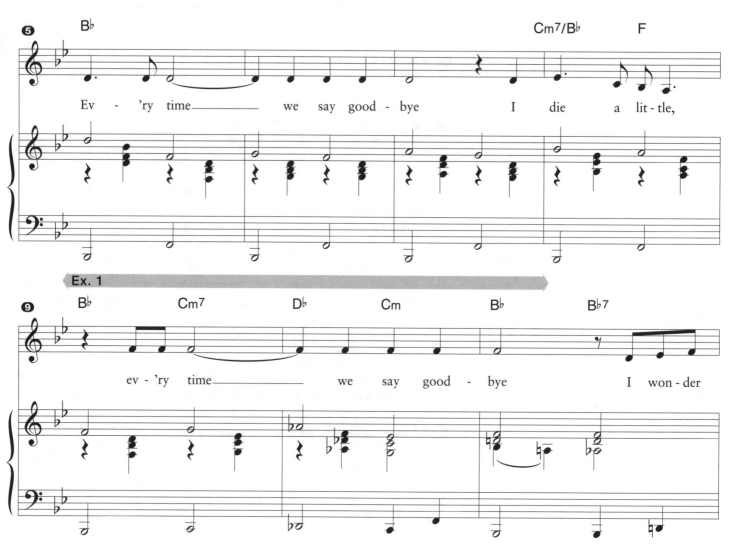

Vocal Notes

Ev'ry Time We Say Goodbye

This song became Ella's signature tune as far as her European fans were concerned, and there was a period when audiences wouldn't let her off stage until she had sung it! Originally written by Cole Porter for the show 'Seven Lively Arts' (1944), it is one of Cole Porter's simplest, most poignant ballads, and Ella's recording shows off the song to perfection. It includes the masterful line – 'There's no love song finer, but how strange the change from major to minor.'

Ella delivers the song with a bitter-sweet mournful quality that perfectly suits the lyric. She manages to get a yearning quality into some of the phrasing, and it's not until you look into the detail of how she does this that you fully appreciate what a master songstress she was. For example, in the line 'ev'ry time we say goodbye' in bars 9, 10 and 11, notice how the smallest of scoops on the syllables 'we', 'say' and '-bye' create a nagging, repetitive sorrow that pervades the texture of the song.

Ex 1 'ev'ry time we say goodbye'

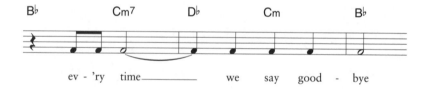

She does the same thing on the line 'think so little of me' in bars 17 and 18, where she underlines the song's beautifully melancholic shift to E♭ minor by tugging emotionally at the notes like a lost child.

Ex 2 'think so little of me'

Ella's use of portamento is usually very reserved, so that when she does use it to any great extent its impact is increased. A good example of this occurs in bar 31 with the immortal lyric 'how strange the change from major to minor'. On the word 'strange' she dive-bombs from the A♭ to the D below, and back up to the G, creating as she does so a perfect 'word painting' of the lyric at this point.

Ex 3 'But how strange the change from major to minor.'

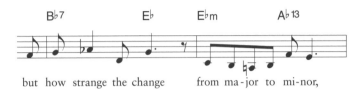

In the following line, 'ev'ry time we say goodbye' (bars 33-35) she emphasises the last, and most poignant, word with two devices. On the first syllable she puts in a scoop from B♭ (the tonic) to C, and she finally settles back on the tonic (B♭) with a little neighbour-note grace note figure. The cumulative effect of this is a kind of delaying oscillation before the final acceptance that the phrase is finished. It's as if she doesn't want to arrive at that final note, that final goodbye.

Ex 4 'Ev'ry time we say goodbye.'

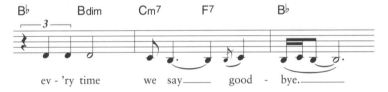

This is very, very subtle word painting. It would be interesting to know how much of it is planned and thought about, and how much is an innate musical response to the lyric and the music. Some may argue that her interpretation is all about feel and isn't in any way planned or thought about. This may be so, but why then would she repeat the same phrasing on the exact same phrases later in the song? Look at bars 47 and 50-51 for the evidence. Either way, the songs are here for us to pick over and to learn from.

TECHNIQUE**tip**

The portamento Ella uses on the word 'strange' on both its appearances in the song isn't merely a slide from one note to another. As with her shake, it is accompanied by a controlled lessening of the vocal tone. To master this technique, try singing the phrase 'but how strange the change', first having listened carefully to exactly how Ella does it. Once you've mastered it in this key, try transposing it to other keys and registers, making sure that your technique is secure across your whole range.

JOHNNY ONE NOTE

Words by Lorenz Hart
Music by Richard Rodgers

Brightly

John-ny could on-ly sing one note, and the note he sang was this.

Ah.

Johnny One Note

Johnny One Note

Vocal Notes

Johnny One Note

Here we see the other side of Ella – the dazzling virtuosity with a show-stopping tour-de-force from the 1936 Rodgers and Hart show 'Babes In Arms'. This song was made famous by Judy Garland in the 1948 MGM musical of the same name. Gone is the gentle, caressing, velvety sound and in its place is a Broadway 'belter' of a voice that could bring any house down. Ella takes to this rôle like a duck to water, showing a few fancy tricks of her own when it comes to fronting a big band.

Technically this song is demanding. The whole vocal line is constructed around two Gs an octave apart, and the singer is required to perform some pretty fancy footwork as the song moves along at a rapid pace.

For example, the singer's first entry in bar five is a repeated rhythmic figure on a low G. This requires clear enunciation and strict adherence to the rhythmic pulse. This is not easy to do in the lower register.

Ex 1 'Johnny could only... sang was this.'

John-ny could on - ly sing one note, and the note he sang was this.

This is immediately followed by a held G an octave above. This note sits in a much stronger register for most singers, so you have to guard against 'belting' this note too much, making your lower register appear weak in comparison.

Notice how Ella adds impact to this long 'Ah' by adding a scoop at the beginning and by pouring on the vibrato. In other words, it's not merely volume that supplies the impact of this note, but carefully applied vocal techniques.

The verse offers up more problems in the same mould. The voice performs an ascending line from C to the G above, but is underpinned with a repeated low

G. So, each bar is effectively an exercise in performing ever-widening intervals from C–G–C to G–G–G. The danger here is that the constantly repeated low G can get lost in your boots as you concentrate on making the upper part of the line.

Ex 2 'sang out with gusto and just overlorded the place.'

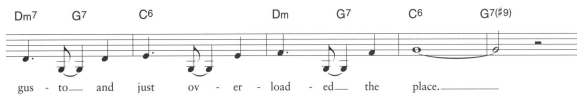

gus - to— and   just   ov - er - load - ed— the   place.————

One characteristic of ascending phrases generally is that they tend to get louder as they go up (and descending ones tend to get quieter too!). It's also only human to 'aim' for the long note at the end of the phrase (on 'place' and 'face'). The combination of these factors can serve to rob the repeated low notes of all their impact, so make sure you keep that low G firmly in your sights as you ascend the big phrase.

This song moves at a fast tempo, but even so some of the phrases are quite long. In order to negotiate them safely your breathing has to be good. Make sure you breathe deeply from the diaphragm before each of these long phrases.

TECHNIQUE**tip**

As you will have gathered, the key to success in this song is to be able to get around the lower and middle ranges of your voice with dexterity and control, all the while maintaining vocal tone. The best way to practise this is to do interval training. Not the kind you do in the gym, but the kind you do at the piano! Pick a note from low in your register, then sing the next note up, and go back again. Now increase the interval to a third, then a fourth and so on, all the time making sure your intonation and tone are good on all notes, not just the upper ones. Gradually increase the speed and, of course, try it in a number of keys and registers. And don't forget to do the reverse too, where you start from a high note and gradually work down.

Makin' Whoopee!

Words by Gus Kahn
Music by Walter Donaldson

Makin' Whoopee!

Vocal Notes

Makin' Whoopee!

This Walter Donaldson/Gus Kahn satire on the sexual imperative was penned for the 1928 musical 'Whoopee!', which became a Hollywood film in 1930. It's a joyously sardonic, tongue-in-cheek look at the eternal tensions between man and woman, from courtship, through marriage, adultery and even divorce. And its central theme is to lay the blame at the door of the honeypot behind every relationship – makin' whoopee!

The song has a light rhythmic feel, and requires a similar treatment of the vocal. There are several key points regarding the shape of the melodic line and its rhythm that will help you shape the phrases. The first thing to notice is that the vocal line is made up of lots of repeated rhythmic phrases that go 'short, short, short, long....'. Indeed this three-note pick up is the most remarkable feature of this song. It is everywhere. Just look at the first phrase and you'll see it happening in every bar!

Ex 1 'Another bride, another June, another sunny honeymoon.'

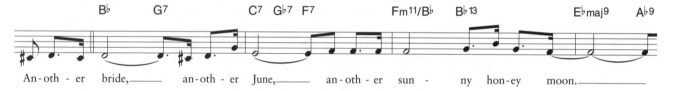

With so much rhythmic repetition it's important to keep the vocal fresh and inventive, so a degree of licence with the written rhythm is to be expected. As this is a swing number don't fall into the trap of singing these dotted rhythms as they are written. Listen to how the vocal is pulled around on the CD to get some idea of what you will need to do. Notice also how Ella bends the words 'season' and 'reason' in exactly the same way in bars nine and 10 to mirror the internal rhyme of the song with this musical device .

Ex 2 'another season. Another reason for makin'...'

To experiment with different feels over the same basic pulse try this exercise. Take a part of the backing track that you feel comfortable with, then practise singing over it in even quavers. Gradually move towards long-short swing combinations, and keep going until you've gone too far the other way, and your singing sounds spiky and straight. Now settle back to somewhere just past the middle until the swing feel sounds right. Now try introducing triplet groupings instead of the written groups of fours. When you feel comfortable with this try alternating triplets with fours. Gradually teach yourself to alternate between these various groupings seamlessly, so that you don't disrupt the flow of the song.

The word 'whoopee!' (bar 11) sees the first big leap in the song – an octave from B♭ to B♭. This has to be delivered in the same light, throw-away style of the rest of the song, so make sure you're prepared for this sudden leap.

The middle eight (bar 21) sees the introduction of another rhythmic figure. Notice again how this two-bar phrase is repeated down a step, making a four-bar phrase, and that this four-bar phrase is then repeated making the entire middle eight out of just one phrase.

Ex 3 'Picture a little love-nest'

Having this much internal repetition within a song is unusual, and you have to vary your approach to the repeated phrases in order to keep the song interesting. Listen carefully to the subtle rhythmic variations Ella uses, and see if you can incorporate some of them into your own performance.

Here are a couple of examples. In bars 25-26 Ella holds back the words 'sweet love-nest' a fraction,

Ex 4 'Picture the same sweet love-nest'

then does the opposite with the following phrase 'think what a year can bring', where she concertinas the front of the phrase into four quavers.

Ex 5 'Think what a year can bring.'

NICE WORK IF YOU CAN GET IT

Music and Lyrics by George Gershwin and Ira Gershwin

Nice Work If You Can Get It

Vocal Notes

Nice Work If You Can Get It

This is a George and Ira Gershwin classic originally written for the RKO movie 'A Damsel In Distress' in 1937. The title of the song was borrowed by Ira from an old Punch cartoon, and it yielded some of the most charming music heard on screen. Not surprisingly it became one of Ella's favourite songs from the GERSHWIN SONG BOOK.

This song gives Ella the chance to show a glimpse of her jazz artistry. She was one of the great 'scat' singers, with a gift for melodic invention and improvisation, and she could really swing! In this song she takes an improvisatory approach to the melody throughout, often decorating phrases with little improvised asides, extending intervals, inverting them, stretching the melody here, contracting it there. Her whole approach creates a freshness and vitality that keeps the song alive, even after many outings.

In the first two phrases (bars 5-12) she plays it pretty straight, giving us the melody as it was written. In the following phrase (bars 13-16) she improvises a beautifully crafted response to 'strolling with the one boy' with a triplet figure in bar 15 and a delayed 'sigh' in bar 16.

Ex 1 'strolling with the one boy, sighing sigh after sigh'

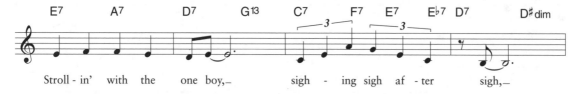

This use of triplets over what is essentially a swing groove is one of Ella's favourite devices, and it crops up all over the place in her jazz work, and it crops up twice more in this short song.

From bar 39 we see her swapping four bar phrases with the pianist. Notice how she takes an element of what he plays to use in her response. In the first example (bars 43-46) she takes the chromatic line from the piano and weaves a chromatic line of her own with the main 'hook' of the song 'nice work if you can get it, and you can get it if you try'.

Ex 2 'Nice work... get it if you only try.'

Ni - ice work if you can get it,—— and you can get it if you on - ly try.

In the second pair of phrases she swaps from a melodic (or harmonic) idea to a rhythmic one. The piano plays a stopped offbeat rhythm on the chromatic line, and Ella responds by modifying it to a triplet figure. She cuts right across what the piano is playing with a bold ascending line, extending (and emphasising) the word 'nice', making it into three syllables!

Ex 3 'Nice work... get it if you only try.'

Ni - i - ice work if you can get it and you can get it if—— you—— try.——

Whatever she does, she's always aware of the structure. Here she only has a four-bar phrase to play with, and she needs to resolve back to the tonic (C) each time. Take a close look at how she does this in both instances. Each is different, but the emphasis of the tonic note itself (not just a chord tone from C major) couldn't be more definite.

She continues this approach throughout the song. Just look at the middle eight (from bar 55) to see how she continues to invent new ways to deliver the material.

TECHNIQUE**tip**

Not all singers feel comfortable improvising, but this is the perfect song in which to start. Using the backing track, take the four-bar phrases in the middle of the song and improvise your own figures. If you know a little about harmony then refer to the chords, but if you don't, use your ears to tell you what works. If you're unsure, start with what Ella does and gradually move away from it, introducing your own ideas one by one. The key to making it work is to listen hard to what the piano is doing. Once you get used to listening 'creatively' as you're singing, your confidence will grow. Then you might like to take this improvisatory approach and apply it to other parts of the song.

SLAP THAT BASS

Music and Lyrics by George Gershwin and Ira Gershwin

Zoom, zoom,— zoom, zoom,— rhy-thm lead your ace.— The

fu-ture does-n't fret me if I can on-ly get me some-one to slap that bass!

Hap - pi - ness is not a rid - dle when I'm list-'ning to—— that big bass

fid - dle.

Slap That Bass   **59**

Repeat to fade

Slap That Bass **63**

Vocal Notes

Slap That Bass

This is another song from the team of George and Ira Gershwin, written for the all-singing, all-dancing film 'Shall We Dance' from the studios of RKO Pictures in 1937. The film starred Fred Astaire and Ginger Rogers, and it was an unwritten rule that a key feature of every Astaire picture of the '30s was a prolonged dance sequence. It didn't necessarily have to have much to do with the film's plot, but it was a big part of the attraction for the many devoted followers that made up the cinema-going public.

The plot of 'Shall We Dance' concerned, amongst other things, a trans-Atlantic voyage. It was a simple matter to drop the dapper Astaire into the ship's boiler room and there allow him to do his stuff against a background of pulsating machinery. For this rhythmic scene the Gershwins wrote *Slap That Bass*, a number in the tradition of, and making sly reference to, *I Got Rhythm*.

Although this is a big band number it's pretty understated, allowing Ella to imbue the song with a lightness and delicacy not usually to be found in such a number. In part this is due to the subject matter – the song is about, and features, the 'bass fiddle' referred to in bar 25. Because of this George Gershwin was faced with a difficult musical problem.

The bass, though providing the foundation of the big band, doesn't cut through the texture of the ensemble like a lead trumpet or drummer, so the ensemble has to be toned down to compensate. Gershwin comes up with a neat solution to this thorny orchestration problem by creating an episodic song, where the horns get to 'shout' in short swing sections. The main feel and texture of the song edges towards a straighter Latin feel, which is understated.

For example, the song starts with solo bass playing an octave-based figure, to which voice is added, contributing its own version of the bass line.

TECHNIQUE tip

Feel and groove are everything in this piece. It's important when you're moving from a half-swung or straight feel to an all-out swing groove that the difference is immediately noticeable. To get a swing groove under your skin you have to listen to the acknowledged masters. Two of the best examples are the virtuosic big band drummer Buddy Rich, and the master of groove, Mr Frank Sinatra. Listen to what they play or sing when they are really swinging and try to lock into their groove, then bring this to your own singing. Listening is some of the most enjoyable and rewarding practice you can do.

Ex 1 'Zoom, zoom, zoom, zoom'

Zoom,   zoom,—   zoom,   zoom,—

In bar 9 the bass starts to 'walk', a swinging line that requires a different feel from the singer as she sings 'politics and taxes… there's no happiness'.

Ex 2 'Politics and taxes… there's no happiness.'

po - li - tics and tax - es   and   peo - ple grind-ing ax-es,   there's no   hap - pi - ness.—

In bar 13 the song reverts to its original straighter feel, and so the mould is set for the rest of the song.   To change feel from phrase to phrase requires good ears and a sympathetic approach to the musicians you're playing with.

Notice the Ella trademark of triplets over a four-based accompaniment in bars 53-54.

Ex 3 'Dictators would be better off if they zoom…'

Dic - ta -tors would   be   bet - ter   off   if   they

Gershwin can't resist the reference to 'I Got Rhythm' in bars 60 and 76, though it raises the question of which song benefits most by the comparison!

Ex 4 'All got rhythm'

all   got   rhy-thm.

Ex 5 'All got rhythm'

all——   got   rhy-thm.

OH, LADY BE GOOD

Music and Lyrics by George Gershwin and Ira Gershwin

Ex. 1

Lis - ten to my tale of woe, it's ter - rib - ly sad but true.

All dressed up, no place to go,— each eve - ning I'm aw - f'ly blue.

Oh, Lady Be Good

Oh, Lady Be Good

Vocal Notes

Oh, Lady Be Good

This is another George and Ira Gershwin number, written for the show 'Lady Be Good' in 1924, and subsequently made into a movie by MGM in 1941. It's a lovelorn ballad which, along with *Fascinating Rhythm*, was a highlight of the show. Interestingly, the show was originally titled 'Black Eyed Susan' until the writers heard what was to become the title song for the first time. This was the musical in which Fred and Adele Astaire starred on Broadway and in London.

This song became one of Ella's biggest hits. She recorded it in 1947 as an up-tempo bop number, racing through the lyric on her way to a breakneck scat solo. It was this recording that did most to establish Ella's jazz image.

Norman Granz had the idea to slow the song down, in what was surely one of the most inspired tempo changes. In the GERSHWIN SONG BOOK she brings unexpected poignancy and meaning to this originally breezy show song. By way of anecdote, it was also reputedly Bing Crosby's favourite song.

The song starts with a colla voce intro which Ella delivers with customary panache. Notice the trademark fast vibrato on 'woe' in bar six and grace note descents to the key words 'sad' and 'true'. Already in the first four bars of her vocal we've had three distinguishing features of Ella's vocal style.

Ex 1 'Listen to my tale of woe, it's terribly sad but true.'

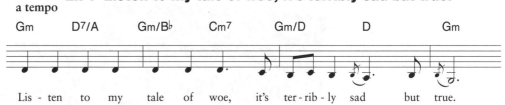

There is a beautiful moment in bars 17-20 where the lyric is hopeful and optimistic ('I could blossom out I know, with somebody just like you'), and George Gershwin pulls a compositional rabbit out of the hat! He moves suddenly to the brighter key of G major for four bars before yanking the song back to its more melancholy home key of B♭. Ella seems to sense that the structure and harmony of the song are doing all the work here, and she delivers the line absolutely straight.

Ex 2 'I could blossom out I know, with somebody just like you.'

The net effect of all this is that when the rhythm section comes in on the home chord of B♭ the song takes on a bitter-sweet melancholic air.

An interesting quirk in her approach to the triplet figures emerges over the next few bars. See how in bars 23 and 25 she decorates not the first, but the second note of each triplet ('lady be good') with a shake. She does the same thing in bars 31 and 33.

At bar 37 see how she pours on the pathos with a few well placed scoops, falls and shakes. After the long mournful 'Oh', which is decorated with a scoop, the 'please' falls away before 'pity' is emphasised with a slow shake that we've notated as semiquavers. It's no coincidence that this is the first line of the song's hook, and Ella pulls out all the stops.

Ex 3 'Oh, please have some pity'

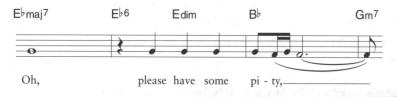